10 Things You Need to Know About

Cliques

by Jen Jones

Consultants:

Patricia Adler
Professor of Sociology
University of Colorado, Boulder

Peter Adler
Professor of Sociology and Criminology
University of Denver, Colorado

Capstone
press

Mankato, Minnesota

Snap Books are published by Capstone Press,
151 Good Counsel Drive, P.O. Box 669, Mankato, Minnesota 56002.
www.capstonepress.com

Library of Congress Cataloging-in-Publication Data
Jones, Jen.
     Cliques / by Jen Jones.
     p. cm. —(Snap books. 10 things you need to know about)
     Summary: "Provides helpful information to understand and deal with cliques during the middle
school years and beyond"—Provided by publisher.
     Includes bibliographical references and index.
     ISBN-13: 978-1-4296-0128-3 (hardcover)
     ISBN-10: 1-4296-0128-0 (hardcover)
     1. Girls—Psychology. 2. Cliques (Sociology) 3. Interpersonal relations in children. 4. Interpersonal
conflict in children. I. Title. II. Series.
HQ777.J65 2008
158.2'508352—dc22   2007001317

Editors: Wendy Dieker and Christine Peterson
Designer: Juliette Peters
Photo Researchers: Charlene Deyle and Jo Miller

Photo Credits:
Corbis/Jim Craigmyle, 17; Corbis/Kevin Dodge, 4–5; Corbis/Little Blue Wolf Productions, 22; fotolia/Jason Stitt, 24–25;
The Image Works/Topham, 9; iStockphoto, back cover, 16, 26; iStockphoto/Jan Rihak, 6, 27; iStockphoto/Loke Yek
Mang, 19; iStockphoto/Sherrianne Talon, 23; Michele Torma Lee, 32; Photri-MicroStock, 11; Shutterstock/@erics, 18;
Shutterstock/Eric Simard, 7; Shutterstock/Jason Stitt, 20–21; Shutterstock/Laurence Gough, 15; Shutterstock/Matthew
Jacques, 21 (bottom right); Shutterstock/Pam Burley, 10; Shutterstock/Ralph Biggor, 14, 30; Shutterstock/Stephen Coburn,
cover; SuperstockInc./age fotostock, 13

1 2 3 4 5 6 12 11 10 09 08 07

Table of Contents

Introduction

Junior high is a time of major change. Your body is changing, and your personality is evolving. You'll probably notice that friendships are way different than before. Gone are the days when everyone had fun together. Suddenly there are all kinds of groups, or cliques. You're not quite sure where you fit in. Some of your friends might join the "popular" group, while others will split off and do their own thing.

If you're faced with some hard choices, you're not alone. Cliques can be found at every school. Whether you're caught in the middle of a clique or feeling alone, this book has an answer for you. Get ready to find your own clique survival style.

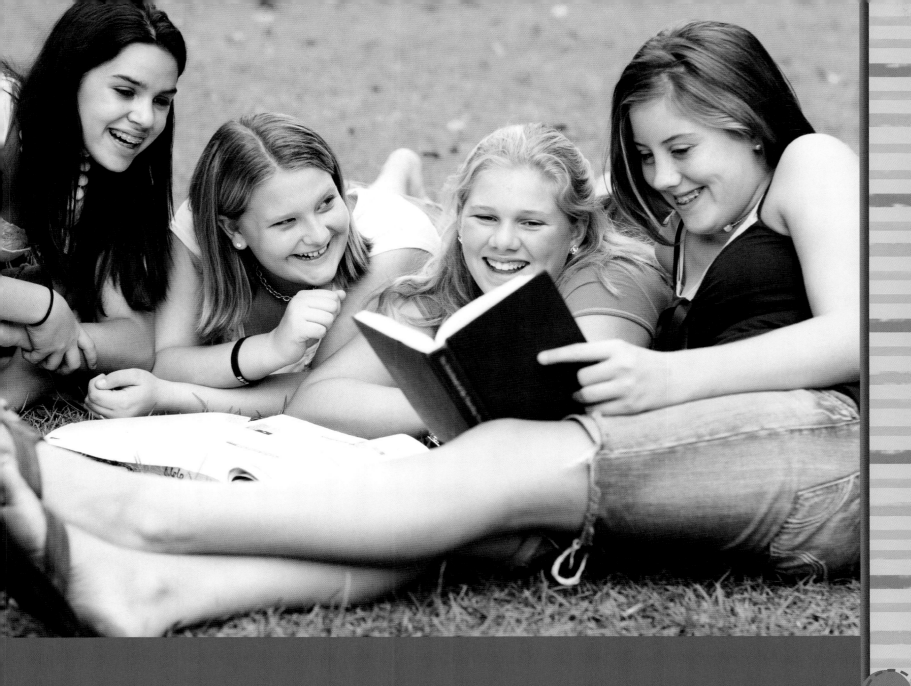

1 There are four kinds of cliques

Simply put, cliques are groups of friends who click. They share the same interests, wear the same style of clothes, and spend most of their time together. Most cliques are closed to outsiders. Members come and go as rules for staying in the group change.

Cliques come in all shapes and sizes. Four kinds of people are most often grouped together:

- The popular kids reach their star status by being confident and outgoing. They thrive in social situations.

- The fringe, or wannabe, crowd tries to be like (or at least liked by) the popular kids.

- A friendship circle gathers because they have something in common, such as drama club or athletics.

- Loners keep to themselves. They often sit alone at school events or keep quiet in class.

Do you see yourself in one of these groups?

2 Cliques have both good and bad sides

Although most cliques exclude others, they aren't all bad. These groups give members a sense of belonging. They can even build super-strong friendship bonds. It feels good to know your friends have got your back. Yet the friendship balance within some cliques is delicate. Saying or doing the "wrong" thing might lead your friends to cut ties with you.

There are other downsides to cliques. Getting too caught up in the group might shut you off from a classmate who is BFF material. You could also lose sight of yourself by trying to fit another person's idea of what's cool. You might even be part of a group that teases or bullies others. In these situations, your personal values are tested. What will you do?

As cliques form, labels take shape

Girls have many sides to their personalities. But girls are often labeled based on just one part of who they are. It's easy to look at a basketball player and label her a "jock." But she might also be a singer or a math whiz. Groups of friends are also lumped into common stereotypes. For instance, kids who play instruments might be labeled "band geeks." Smart types who hang out together might be branded "nerds."

Take a minute before you label people based on the clubs they join or the clothes they wear. Being a cheerleader doesn't make a girl mean or an airhead. Take a closer look and get to know what others are really about. Wouldn't you want people to do the same for you?

4 Cliques have a "follow the leader" mentality

In the 2004 movie *Mean Girls*, Lindsay Lohan plays "Cady." She's a new girl who gets pulled into an ironclad clique and becomes a catty clone. The flick was based on the book *Queen Bees and Wannabes*. In the book, author Rosalind Wiseman explores clique dynamics. She believes every clique has a "queen bee," or powerful leader. A queen bee sets the tone for the rest of the group. She expects things to be done her way.

When you belong to a queen bee's hive, it's easy to become a wannabe. After all, queen bees know the secret to popularity, so you want to be like them. You might try to dress or act just like a queen bee. But in becoming a clone, you lose yourself in the process.

Every school has its own version of cool. In some cases, the athletes rule the school. In others, smart kids reign supreme. Some kids try to play down their skills or assets to create a more acceptable image. For instance, an ace at algebra might play dumb in class to avoid being singled out. A talented musician may drop out of band if the popular crowd suddenly decides that playing an instrument is "uncool."

This behavior can create serious problems. Failing tests on purpose could keep a student from getting into college. Dropping out of band could short change a promising future in music. Embrace your talents and you'll be sure to shine.

6 Cliques have a revolving door

Friendship is like the weather. It can be tough to forecast the future. Stormy times and changing conditions can create a major case of "Friend Today, Gone Tomorrow." Three friends who used to be peas in a pod can suddenly become three's a crowd. A misunderstanding or fight can permanently change the group's makeup. These shake-ups often come down from clique leaders. They control who gets to be in the mix.

When your clique turns against you, it hurts. It's painful to see your former friends having fun and pretending you don't exist. While these alliances are a fact of clique life, you can survive with your dignity in one piece.

Trusty Tips

If you feel left out in the cold, try these tips on for size:

❁ Explore your feelings by talking with a trusted friend or parent, or by writing in a journal.

❁ Confront the issue head-on. Give your friends a chance to explain why they're angry, and try to talk out the problem.

❁ Seek out a new support system. Look for friends who aren't as quick to judge or ignore you.

❁ Keep your head held high. Your former friends lose their "power" if their actions seem like they don't affect you.

7 Being popular isn't all it's cracked up to be

Ever heard the old saying, "The grass is always greener on the other side?" Applied to popularity, that saying just might be true. Sure, it looks like the in-crowd is having a blast, but don't always believe what you see. Popular kids often wonder if people like them for who they really are, or just because of their social status.

Being popular also carries a lot of pressure. Popular kids might feel they have to drink, smoke, or even do drugs to keep their place in the group. They might also feel pressure to maintain a certain appearance. As a result, they may feel pressure to buy clothes they can't afford or pick up unhealthy eating habits. Remember, life in the cool crowd is far from perfect.

8 Cliques don't end after graduation

Growing up is a fact of life, and like it or not, so are cliques. After graduating from high school, you'll find many exclusive groups. Most college campuses are home to sororities and fraternities. These exclusive clubs for girls and guys have stiff rules about getting in the group and staying there. Many adults form cliques with coworkers or neighborhood pals.

You might groan at the thought of never escaping cliques. But as time passes, you'll learn to handle social situations. After all, adults rely less on what others think. They are confident in their own decisions. You'll value different qualities as you age. Suddenly, it will be cool to be super-smart or speak your mind.

Geek to Chic

Ever wonder why *Princess Diaries* author Meg Cabot is so good at writing for young girls? She remembers all too well what it was like. A self-proclaimed nerd, Meg says she was hopelessly uncool as a kid. Today, her books top best-seller lists and she attends the same social events as authors like J. K. Rowling. Revenge of the nerds, indeed!

9 Breaking the clique mold

No one is perfect. We've all made mistakes or treated someone poorly. Yet it's never too late to make a change. It's easy to branch out from your social circle. Do your own thing. Break away from the negative aspects of cliques and help others to do the same.

Here are some ideas on how to do just that:

- A simple smile or "hello" goes a long way. Make the effort to reach out to new people in the hallways.

- Don't put up with bullying. Standing up for yourself and others will make you feel good inside, and it could change someone's life.

- Step out of your comfort zone. Join a new school activity or spend time with friends who don't go to your school.

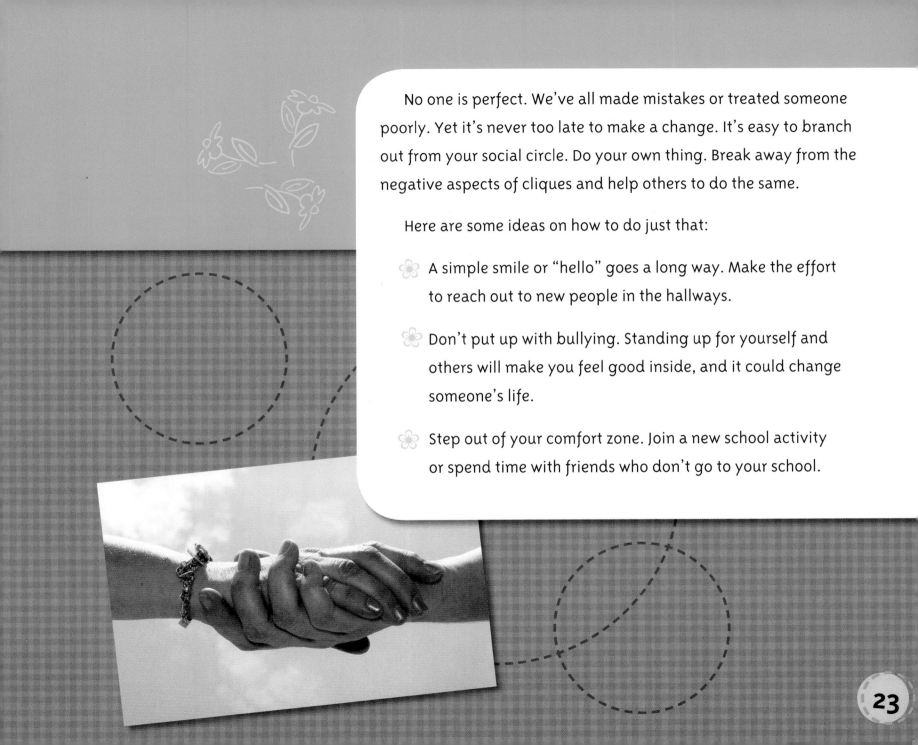

10 One doesn't have to be the loneliest number

Whether you're part of a clique or not, it's normal to feel alone sometimes. Knowing how to deal with loneliness will help you get through the hard times. One way to break through loneliness and clique politics is to be a "drifter." Their confidence attracts friends from all across the social board. Drifters are nice to everyone and aren't afraid of what others think.

If you're not a drifter, there are other ways you can deal with loneliness. In any situation, have the courage to be yourself. Letting go of the pressure to be accepted can be very freeing. You don't have to copy the popular kids to fit in. People enjoy spending time with friends who are confident and unique. Use your individuality and don't be afraid to stand out in a crowd.

A Few More Things You Need to Know

The seeds for cliques were planted hundreds of years ago

In ancient Rome, people were divided into social groups based on their wealth, politics, and jobs. That trend still continues today. Sometimes being accepted at school can mirror your place in society. In fact, some experts say wealth is one of the top three deciding factors for popularity.

Social sites are the online cliques

Some people go online to escape the real world. Yet clique behavior is just as common online. Sites like MySpace and Facebook let users approve or deny friend requests.

Popularity means different things

Research shows that popularity means different things for guys and girls. Guys often value athletic ability, masculinity, and even height. For girls, looks and fashion often decide who's popular.

Cliques can have dangerous outcomes

When kids are treated like outcasts, they often feel angry, humiliated, or helpless. In some cases, this leads them to take revenge against their peers. Sadly, school violence is often a result of this problem. If you feel someone is really upset, share your concerns with a teacher or parent.

Hollywood is fascinated by cliques

From '80s flicks like *The Breakfast Club* to more recent hits like *Mean Girls*, Hollywood has always put the spotlight on cliques. Many films have explored the social jungles of high school. Today's pop culture landscape is no different, except that much of the drama is unscripted. Reality shows like *Laguna Beach* give an inside look at real-life cliques and queen bees.

Quiz

What's Your Clique Survival Style?

Your gym teacher asks you to pick partners. You choose:
- **A** Your BFF—who else?
- **B** Someone who you're not embarrassed to be seen with
- **C** Whoever is standing closest to you

The clique situation at your school:
- **A** Is what makes showing up every day so fun
- **B** Is a necessary evil
- **C** Is out of control

A friend has been acting weird all day. What do you do?
- **A** Text message all your other friends to see if they know what's up
- **B** Inwardly freak out
- **C** Ask her for an explanation

At the family dinner table, you're most likely to talk about:
- **A** Who you want to ask to the school dance
- **B** What the queen bee did at school today
- **C** The upcoming English test

You're a chess wiz. Joining the club would be:
- **A** A social disaster
- **B** A horrible idea unless your friends joined too
- **C** A lot of fun

Your friends are going shopping, but you don't really feel like joining them. You:
- **A** Talk them into coming over instead
- **B** Go anyway
- **C** Do your own thing

You hear a nasty rumor about a classmate. What do you do?
- **A** Who cares? You don't have time for boring outsiders.
- **B** Ask the other clique members if they've heard it yet
- **C** Keep quiet; you don't want a part in spreading rumors

Your BFF has been spending a lot of time with someone else, and you're starting to feel like a third wheel. What's your reaction?

A Two can play that game—you find your own new best friend

B Silently stew and go along with it

C Talk to her about your feelings

How good are you at keeping secrets?

A Where's the nearest megaphone?

B Depends whose secret it is

C They'll follow me to the grave.

There's a new girl at school. What's your approach?

A Size her up to see if she could be competition.

B Watch to see if everyone else likes her

C Invite her to sit at your lunch table.

A classmate doesn't invite you to her b-day party. What do you do?

A Talk all your friends out of going.

B Start sucking up—you want that invite.

C Don't sweat it. You can make plans with other friends.

You spot a friend flirting with your crush. You:

A Cozy up to her ex

B Turn up your own flirt factor a notch

C Remind her later about your feelings

What's your ideal Saturday night?

A Throwing an exclusive shindig

B A night out with the girls

C A movie and some Ben & Jerry's with your BFF

What would you be voted in the yearbook?

A Most Popular

B Biggest Party Girl

C Most Likely to Succeed

Which description fits you best?

A Queen Bee

B Wannabe

C Drifter

When scoring your answers, A equals 5 points, B equals 3 points, and C equals 1 point. Total them up and find out your clique survival style!

1-25 = Catty clique behavior is no match for your strong personality and independent style. You avoid silly dramas and fussy fights.

26-50 = SOS! You're in danger of becoming a clone. You have a mind of your own; it's time to start using it.

51-75 = Always the center of attention, you pride yourself on being the leader of the pack. Be careful not to abuse your power.

Glossary

dignity (DIG-nuh-tee)—a quality that makes people worthy of honor or respect

dynamic (dye-NAM-ik)—the changing atmosphere of a group

exclude (ek-SKLOOD)—to keep someone from joining or taking part in something

humiliate (hyoo-MIL-ee-ate)—to make someone look or feel foolish or embarrassed

individuality (in-duh-vij-oo-AL-uh-tee)—the qualities that set a person apart from others

stereotype (STER-ee-oh-tipe)—an overly simple picture or opinion of a person, group, or thing

value (VAL-yoo)—beliefs or ideas that are important to a person

Read More

Criswell, Patti Kelley. *Friends: Making Them & Keeping Them.* Middleton, Wis.: Pleasant Company Publications, 2006.

Koubek, Christine Wickert. *Friends, Cliques, and Peer Pressure: Be True to Yourself.* Teen Issues. Berkeley Heights, N.J.: Enslow, 2002.

Moehn, Heather. *Everything You Need to Know About Cliques.* The Need to Know Library. New York: Rosen, 2001.

Powell, Jillian. *Self-esteem.* It's Your Health. North Mankato, Minn.: Smart Apple Media, 2006.

Internet Sites

FactHound offers a safe, fun way to find Internet sites related to this book. All of the sites on FactHound have been researched by our staff.

Here's how:
1. Visit *www.facthound.com*
2. Choose your grade level.
3. Type in this book ID **1429601280** for age-appropriate sites. You may also browse subjects by clicking on letters, or by clicking on pictures and words.
4. Click on the **Fetch It** button.

FactHound will fetch the best sites for you!

31

About the Author

As a former cheerleader and drama club member, Jen Jones experienced her fair share of drama in school—on and off the stage.

She is a Los Angeles-based writer who has published stories in magazines such as *American Cheerleader*, *Dance Spirit*, *Ohio Today*, and *Pilates Style*. She has also written for E! Online and PBS Kids. Jones has been a Web site producer for major talk shows such as *The Jenny Jones Show*, *The Sharon Osbourne Show*, and *The Larry Elder Show*. She recently completed books on cheerleading, knitting, figure skating, and gymnastics.

Index